Confessions of a Pitch Consultant

What They Don't Teach You At Sales Academy

Elliot Epstein

To Noel Speering

Every guru was once a kid
who knew nothing.

WHAT PROFESSIONAL SALES LEADERS and SALES PEOPLE SAY ABOUT 'CONFESSIONS OF A PITCH CONSULTANT.'

'I love these insights.'

'Funny…irreverent…can't stop laughing.'

'Real life stories.'

'Awesome ideas.'

'Great guidance for Sales Leaders.'

'Thank you…as a sales manager, it gives me interesting ideas to challenge myself with.'

'Spot-on content.'

'Always love how well articulated and right these ideas are.'

'*Scary Sixth Sense of Selling* – a comprehensive course in How to Sell in one article…Brilliant!'

'I got more RELEVANT advice within that one article than in any other formal sales training I have sat through via four global organisations over 15 years.'

ABOUT THE AUTHOR

'The Sales Expert Other Speakers Recommend'

Elliot Epstein, CEO of Salient Communication, is a leading Australian sales expert, pitch consultant and speaker, helping clients win new business in highly competitive markets. He has coached and trained over 4500 people to differentiate, including CEOs, directors, successful sales teams, pre-sales gurus and corporate speakers throughout Australasia and Asia including Hong Kong and Singapore.

Elliot is a dynamic, direct and humorous presenter having spoken at over 900 conferences, training workshops and break-out sessions for leading global companies such as HP, Computershare, SEEK, Hitachi, Toyota, EMC and Telstra.

His no holds barred approach to creatively tackling issues that affect revenue performance, such as selling to large corporates and selling through Procurement have helped clients 'win the unwinnable' for over 15 years.

'Elliot Epstein works with many top 100 Australian companies, high profile sports people and BRW Fast 100 companies, improving everything about the way they sell, negotiate and present.'

- BRW

Foreword

In your career, you will probably have explored all manner of sales blogs, training courses, coaching sessions, boring mission statement meetings, tiring value proposition round tables and group Kumbaya conferences.

You may even have been sober for some of them.

This book is designed for people who want fresh, creative ideas to persuade corporate clients to choose their company rather than that idiot up the road.

It's also for people who are focused on what it takes to seriously win as opposed to taking themselves too seriously.

'Confessions of a Pitch Consultant' is comprised of the most talked about articles I've published on my www.salientcommunication.com.au blog plus a few new, exclusive ones.

So, if you are a Sales Manager, Sales Director, BDM, Account Manager, Relationship Manager, Pre- Sales Guru, Technical Sales Specialist, Solution Architect, Head of Sales, or Superintendent of Customer Experience, then you have a lovely title.

You might also enjoy the approaches in this book that have helped people win the unwinnable, keep their jobs, grow their careers, pay their mortgages and still have time to see their family because they don't have to worry about achieving their budget.

To my clients, thank you for the hundreds of heart-warming testimonials you have kindly left for these articles. I never actually thought they would have a real impact on bottom line results until I received this from a seasoned corporate salesperson:

'I got more RELEVANT advice within that one article than in any other formal sales training I have sat through via four global organisations over 15 years.'

These are my confessions from consulting on thousands of sales engagements and pitches.

Elliot

TABLE OF CONTENTS

I

AUTHENTICITY

Why the real You matters so much

1. SELLING IN AN AUSTRALIAN VOICE

'The Australian is one of the few free men left on this earth. He fears no one, crawls to no one, bludges on no one, and acknowledges no master. Learn his way. Learn his language...you will enter a world that you never dreamed existed. And once you have entered it, you will never leave it.'

- John O'Grady

For a hard-working, resilient, fun-loving nation, we Aussies have not exactly led the world in innovation.

Yes...we have pockets of ground breaking success such as the Cochlear Implant, Penicillin, the Pacemaker and even the Wi-Fi you're using right now.

But we don't have a Silicon Valley or an Israeli Technology Culture.

So, we import stuff like Ikea furniture, European cars and...sales methodologies.

We deploy these methodologies despite a glaring mismatch between the natural, conversational Aussie style of communication and the prescriptive methods these techniques and templates recommend.

We do not have the formality of France, Germany or even the UK.

We do not inherently have the 'control the sale' mentality of Donald Trump's America.

We also do not have the hierarchies and reverence of China, Singapore, Japan or Korea.

So, why would we change our language, style and approach simply because we're engaged in selling?

In fact, we should be exporting our conversational style to the world because in B2B sales today, clients are sicker than the Donald's hair at being pushed, challenged and sausage machined to buy.

Those of you who have been through one of my Salient Programs know that it is liberating, exciting, natural and engaging for clients when you speak like a real human being rather than sounding like the late Stephen Hawking reading a sales playbook.

Clients don't want your canned, qualifying questions – they know what you're trying to do.

They don't want your hubris when you tell them you know better when they have 25 years' experience in their own industry.

They want someone they can trust to listen (and I don't mean for buying signals).

They want someone who can pitch an idea only when it's in full context of the client's overall success.

They want someone who says 'Mate, you haven't got enough budget to do what you really need to do' as opposed to 'I'll see what I can do on the price to get it over the line.'

They want someone who is authentic, not doing a really good job of pretending to be authentic.

I'm calling it AUSthenticity. Now, that's not only going to help you win business wherever you are in the world; it's worth bottling and exporting.

2. BAD SALES

'To be yourself in a world that is constantly trying to make you something else is the greatest accomplishment.'

- Ralph Waldo Emerson

There's a whole genre of *Bad* movies such as Bad Santa, Bad Grandpa, Bad Teacher, Bad Neighbours and the most recent, Bad Moms (genuinely funny!).

The premises vary ranging from absurd stupidity to hilariously heart-warming, but one of the keys to their box office success (collectively over $1 billion) is that people relate to the stereotype being broken.

We don't see ourselves as robotic stereotypes, and whilst people often crave acceptance from their peers or managers, it is not sought at the expense of losing intrinsic individuality.

One of the greatest advantages of selling or consulting is to engage authentically and frequently with other Homo sapiens.

However the trend towards homogenised sales approaches, skills, account plans, recruitment and training is getting worse, not better.

Recently I have conducted five different executive level selling programs and one of my longstanding themes of 'It's

OK to be yourself, rather than being a life support system for a sales methodology' has never resonated so strongly.

After all, you got the job for a reason.

The look of relief, liberation and transformation is palpable as professional sales people discover that the person they are with friends and family is the same person they can be with clients.

The only change is a business context.

The meth(odology) pushers are still selling dangerous pills that destroy creativity, ingenuity, individuality and, ultimately, confidence.

Sales managers reach for more pills to give sales people in an effort to produce results. Sales steroids are legal though, and many are subjected to three and four day regimes to be indoctrinated in the latest sales meth lab.

Unsurprisingly, sales people come out of these labs slightly giddy, heads spinning, temporarily euphoric, only to crash in front of real clients when the alignment of the methodology to their individuality is about as neat as Trump's hair in a tornado.

We need a WADA – an anti-doping program to stop turning wonderfully imperfect, highly competent, individual, introvert, extrovert, ambivert sales people into dopes.

We need to coach, mindful of the individual preferences of real people who deal with real clients.

Standardisation is lazy. It's like emailing sales teams with this week's key sales messages instead of discussing it with them.

It's not 1977 where we only had two flavours of yoghurt. One size fits all sales processes leave a chunk of people wearing ill-fitting suits in front of clients.

Those clients can tell, and that's the bottom line. They're subjected to sales meth addicts daily and they can see exactly what you're doing: Spinning, Challenging or Snapping to try and lead them to buy your widgets.

They're over it.

They want more.

They want the real you.

As Nietzsche said, 'You have your way. I have my way. As for the right way, the correct way, and the only way, it does not exist.'

3. WHY YOUR SALES METHODOLOGY IS STIFLING SUCCESS

"I've been to paradise but I've never been to me.'

- Charlene D'Angelo

US Comedian Jerry Seinfeld suggested that the tuxedo must have been invented by women on the premise that 'Men are all the same, might as well dress them the same.'

Unfortunately too many sales methodologies are based on similar thinking, and if the tuxedo comment is sexist, I'm going to coin the phrase 'Sales-ist.'

Like ice cream flavours, depending on your preference, you can choose a methodology that's designed to build consensus or challenge decision makers or be customer-centric, be solution-centric, seller led, buyer led, forecast led, focused on large accounts, mid-tier accounts or even baby bear accounts.

You choose, Goldilocks!

Now many of you will have your favourites and swear by them, as is often the case when people feel it's the methodology that has made them successful.

Whilst there are a lot of good principles in different methodologies, I think it's more about you.

After 17 years consulting on 'how to differentiate and win' I've coached thousands of people, including the philosopher, the ego-head, the dyslexic, the self-assured, the intellectual, the Year 10 dropout, the OCD, the introvert, the impostor, the sycophant, the drug addict, the 4 times divorced, the driven, the lazy, the unflinchingly decent and the self-esteem bandits.

They're called human beings.

Each one has their own personal and professional background that they bring to the sales process and client engagement.

This is where there is still too much sheep dipping no matter how many times you see 'tailored' in the workbooks.

My mobile phone plan is tailored just for me too....just as I also believe Giselle Bundchen will be interested in me some day.

So, unless you have 5000 reps selling soft drink, where a standardised methodology is a good thing, what are the options for you to develop consistent sales success in B2B sales?

People learn from doing, not watching, so here are three things you can do.

1. Only learn on live deals. Frameworks that use historical data are less relevant to future success. Discuss, coach and guide on real opportunities where the sales person

has a real voice on what's going on and there's a chance to do something about it.

Focus on the steps that are most relevant to that client at this particular moment in time. So what if they skipped step 3 in the process if it wasn't the key issue?

2. There is more than one way to win a deal. Look around the office. Jacinta sells very differently than Nathan, right? Learn from both. Leverage all the internal skills and opinions to see how real business is won.

    •   Some sales managers say 'Jacinta is too reliant on relationships and Nathan is too technical – we need to change this and stick to a formula.'

    •   Do we? Or do we just add new creative approaches, skills and ideas into the mix and coach them to try them rather than change who they are?

    •   My Year 10 dropout, for example, still said 'Youse' and hated filling in sales process sheets…not overly professional, but her success was borne out of courage in going deep across all decision makers and her understanding of her client's real needs was outstanding.

    •   My intellectual philosopher was considered a 'wanker' by some colleagues and he would reference Nietzche in his sales frameworks. Yet he had a laser-like ability to dissect the commerciality of the deal so that clients clearly understood the whole story.

3. Too much process stifles creativity: The left field ideas, the courageous ideas, the game changers, the work to massively differentiate as opposed to producing flaccid sales messages is limited in rigid (*tailored*) methodology.

Finally, a voice from the customer.

After interviewing and befriending many Chief Procurement Officers and senior decision makers I discovered a little known game they play.

It's called 'Guess the methodology.'

Yes, these people who get pitched to every week have to do something to overcome the tedium of self indulgent meetings and poor presentations, so they grab a coffee and try to guess what the sales person has been trained in and then predict what's going to happen next.

Hours of fun!

It doesn't help you differentiate, though.

Amidst the noise of competition and sales messages out there, authentic, creative, human conversations focused on the client are the differentiator.

Combined with creative, fresh ideas and coaching, your human-ness is your differentiator.

As Oscar Wilde said, 'Be yourself, everybody else is already taken.'

II

IT'S NOT ABOUT YOU

What Is Real Client Focus?

4. SCARY SIXTH SENSE OF SELLING

'I see dead deals.'

It's been over 15 years since Bruce Willis walked around in *The Sixth Sense* not realising he was already dead. (Apologies to anyone under 25 who may not have seen one of the most famous twists in movie history.)

In that time, an eerie sixth sense has developed.

'I see dead deals…'

Deals that have all the persuasion of a local government councillor discussing bin night, deals that involve an audience as big as Carols by Candlelight but not the real decision maker and deals that are really exciting for the seller but are on par with cleaning the oven for the client.

But one of the key reasons for new business dropping off like the Aussie Dollar is related to another sense.

It's not taste, sight, hearing, smell or touch.

It's the sense ….of entitlement.

Despite 400 Petabytes of data being written about how true persuasion puts the client at the centre of the call, there are still a lot of people who feel entitled to drive, pitch and talk a lot in client meetings.

It's not about you. Get over it. Sell your ego on eBay while it's still got currency.

Here's a true story that crossed my desk (everyone says that – nothing actually crosses my desk except coffee stains).

It happened on Remembrance Day – November 11.

In the middle of a 10.30 meeting with a potential supplier, a client mentioned that he had family ties back to World War One and would like to observe a minute's silence at 11.00 am to remember the fallen who had fought for our country.

At precisely 11.00 am they stopped talking, bowed their heads slightly and remained silent.

As the client's head came up a minute later, our intrepid sales guy said 'So, given you've had time to reflect for a bit just now, did you think about the proposal we were discussing?'

I believe that guy is now working for NASA circumnavigating Pluto without a space suit… or shuttle.

The initial reaction to such insensitive crappery is to laugh it off with incredulity and a side order of 'What a moron.'

But hang on a second….

How did it even occur to him that his proposal was the central theme of the meeting?

Perhaps because he felt he was entitled. After all, the client agreed to meet him.

Granted, this idiot is off the scale. But how many of us are keen to steer the conversation back to our company, our proposal, our story, regardless of what the client says?

We are all taught and told to listen to the point where the word itself sounds trite and there are eye-rolling sighs of 'Yeah, yeah…listen to the client's needs and then offer something of value back- Wow, you're a guru, Elliot, what an original concept.'

But time after time we don't, because:

- We're keen to get our own three messages across
- We think we've only got one meeting to tell them everything
- We don't like what the client is saying
- We were taught to look for buying signals and jump in at the first opportunity to present our ideas
- We want to qualify them and ask them our prescriptive questions
- We've got budget to get and we need to talk to tell the client what we want him/her to buy

We are not entitled to NOT listen.

Deeply, conversationally, with empathy, with pauses, with care and without an agenda. I see people on 240% of budget because they genuinely listen to everything the client says, every single time.

I see dead deals because the client doesn't feel heard.

5. SALES STOCKHOLM SYNDROME

'I work well with others when you leave me the hell alone.'

In 1973, a bank in Stockholm was held up by armed robbers who kept employees hostage for six days. However, upon release, rather than denouncing these violent thugs, many of the bank's employees felt empathy and an emotional attachment to their captors, often defending their actions.

During the Sydney Lindt Café Siege Inquest, one survivor of the Martin Place tragedy described the deranged perpetrator, Monis, saying 'He was giving us water, he gave us food. I thought it was manipulation but I believed him that he was nice.'

As you may know, these positive feelings towards the criminals were defined by psychiatrist Frank Ochberg as 'Stockholm Syndrome.'

Back to the more sanguine world of business development, Stockholm Syndrome is alive and well and potentially costing you significant revenue and margin.

So, who is most at risk?

- Major Account Managers with one or more massive accounts
- Global or Government Account Directors
- On Site Project Managers/On Site Solution Experts
- Sales Support or Managers of 'House' Accounts

What happens is many of these people spend so much time in one account, often having a desk there, attending all their meetings or on the phone 17 times a day that they forget who the vendor is and who the client is.

The attachment to the client and the empathy for their goals often leads to conflicts of interest where the account manager professing to be the 'client advocate' ends up doing a disservice to the company that won the business and actually pays their salary.

Here are a few examples:

'I sat in their planning meeting last week, there's no more budget.'

'There was an annoying $35k credit hanging over that last project and I agreed with them that we didn't execute properly, so I took it out of the system.'

'All my government clients are in caretaker mode soon, so we'll just have to hang tight for three or four months.'

'I can't present that alternative solution yet, because they've got me working through the business case to maintain the existing platform.'

'I know our contract is up for renewal, but they're pretty pissed at the moment about our CEO leaving, so I'd leave it alone for a bit.'

Insights from client attached account managers are valuable, but they should be taken as just one factor in maximising the relationship, revenue and margin your company needs to achieve.

As you consider how these situations might be managed in your business, I'll leave you with a quote from one of the most famous victims of Stockholm Syndrome, heiress Patty Hearst, who said:

'I mean, they call it Stockholm Syndrome…and, you know, I had no free will. I had virtually no free will, until I was separated from them for about two weeks.'

6. AGENDA BENDER

'For the most part people are not curious except about themselves.'

- John Steinbeck, The Winter of Our Discontent

I often wonder if people who bake, design buildings or make furniture are as inundated as sales people with 1001 ideas that will guarantee them success.

According to sage advice, we should challenge but be empathic, smile a lot, use the CRM, target whales, strategise, post stuff online, tweet, fill the account plan and present like a TED Talker all before lunch time on Wednesday, and then if that doesn't work, cut the arse out of the price at quarter's end, go home and do a combined yoga/Pilates/mindfulness course whilst listening to Sia.

Really?

How about we just have a conversation with clients without an agenda? They will love you for it.

Many people talk about being consultative but it's simply not true. The truth is they want the agenda to be consultative about their special yellow handled widgets.

Others talk of solution selling or challenging the status quo to 'shake the tree' and fifteen other vomitous, meaningless clichés that the Sales Jargonator created.

Psychologists don't have an agenda. The good ones that is, as opposed to the ones in the paper caught on camera horizontal folk dancing with patients.

Psychologists simply want to understand what's going on at a deeper level and they are not looking to steer you into signing up for a three year contract.

They have five times the questioning skills of most sales people. That's why we coach people with these naturally emotive ways of connecting rather than prescribed agenda based questioning.

Agendas are like the Titanic. They are inflexible, often run by control freaks, and are not very good at sidestepping icebergs.

People who go in with an agenda are already leading the client, and the client is wary because they've seen it all before and they'll only reveal what they want to reveal and absolutely nothing more.

You can have general topics the client is interested in such as supply chain certainty, cost reduction or revenue growth, but that's it.

Leave the agenda, pitch, slide pack, leading questions and other old school sales habits in the car....in the sun....and let them rot.

A conversation implies that the discussion could go anywhere and you should revel in being the water skier behind the boat going with them.

'Tell me more, Why , Pausing' are just three legitimate conversation behaviours among the 15 we coach to establish whether there is a professional gain for both parties.

Notice they are 1-3 words, not convoluted, rambling sales questions.

It won't be long before the client is asking you lots of questions and you're on your way.

The nervous bed-wetters out there will no doubt be quite uncomfortable with meetings without agendas because of the control issue (see 'Low Self Esteem').

They worry that sales people will have a lot of coffee chats with no professional purpose. It must be remembered that most clients today are time poor and they didn't agree to the meeting because they want to waste time. They want the conversation, just without the self-indulgent bits.

You don't need a three hour brainstorm and agenda to ask for a meeting. Just ask or tell them you've done some cool stuff in their industry.

When you get there, forget you even mentioned it - they probably have. Then start the psychologist session, getting to the stories of your successes only if and when it comes up.

Finally, Face Time is not an app.

Face to face time with clients is sadly reducing; partly because of the demands of internal CRM, forecasting and account management, but often because it's easier to email, text, Google and get stuck in front of a screen getting distracted by Kim Kardashian's oiled butt than focus on meeting live people.

A psychologist doesn't diagnose or counsel over email.

The top sales performers today are out there, differentiating themselves face to face every day, without self-serving agendas, communicating, conversing and connecting with clients when others are still trying to come up with a detailed agenda to drive a meeting.

Just like Kim's baby oil company, they've got this covered.

7. A MIDSUMMER NIGHT'S SALES DREAM

'Are you sure that we are awake? It seems to me that yet we sleep, we dream'   - William Shakespeare

Nick is an enterprise sales guy, married to Helena, a clinical psychologist.

It is a Thursday, 5.13 am at their house, 14 Theseus Court in the heart of a suburb with 15 organic coffee shops.

Nick wakes up screaming.

Helena: Hey, hey, hey…what's wrong with you…it's still early.

Nick: I had a shocking dream…did you turn the air-con off…it's 38 degrees.

Helena: I was cold…so, come on, you know I love a good nightmare…what happened?

Nick: I was meeting with a CEO and it was just me and him in a really small office and I couldn't shut up. I just kept talking and pitching idea after idea and sharing all the new product updates. It went on for what seemed like hours.

Helena: So, what did he do?

Nick: He said I was very knowledgeable and that he was very interested….and then he rang me straight after this ridiculously long meeting and told me he was giving the business to another company whose Sales Director was a mute.

Helena: A mute... as in couldn't speak?

Nick: Yeah, apparently he had his tongue cut out by his first boss after talking too much in his initial calls with clients....it was awful.

Helena: Then what happened?

Nick: The CEO said 'But I want you to come back tomorrow for a de-brief'....I did and we walked into an even smaller room and he said 'Watch this!'

Helena: Watch what?

Nick: He made me sit through 325,000 slides, the same number as my monthly target, going on about the history of his company and all their divisions and departments. It was excruciating. When I got home you greeted me with a Zimmer frame and said 'Well, aren't you going to give me a kiss for my hundredth birthday?'

Helena: How'd I look?

Nick: Like your mother...only with no teeth.

Helena: Charming! So do you want me to unravel the dream for you?

Nick: I suppose it's just the constant feed of how not to sell on LinkedIn, which I already know anyway... and that leftover goat's cheese from last night.

Helena: Not quite, Nick. It's actually a bit deeper than that.

You do indeed know how to have a conversation with senior executives, listen and let the discussion unfold… that's why you've been successful…plus you've picked up all of my clinical psychology techniques that encourage people to reveal themselves.

But recently, you've been inundated with mixed messages from Head Office. You had the Regional Sales Kick-Off with a whole day of product updates and the cult-like fervour of what you should now be pitching with the new system. You then had the divisional off-site function where the product gurus pummelled you with even more slides and a director who told you and the team to lead all calls with the new presentation.

It's called cognitive dissonance – the disconnect between your attitude and your behaviour. Your dream simply highlights that you have a choice to make. Be true to yourself in the brilliantly conversational way you engage clients or become some weird hybrid that flips between what you do well and the information dumping approach to which you've been exposed.

I guess, your dream is telling you to choose.

Nick: Thanks, honey…don't worry, I've made my choice. I know who I am and what works.

You know we still have an hour before we have to get up…cuddle?

Helena: It's too hot.

8. THE GREATEST DECISION MAKER IN THE WORLD

'Nature is nothing but the inner voice of self-interest.'

- Charles Baudelaire

James was sitting in the coffee shop with his sales manager, Sophie, preparing for their meeting upstairs on Level 31.

Sophie: 'Today, I'm going to introduce you to the greatest decision maker of all time.'

James: 'Who, Donald Trump?'

Sophie: 'Funny....You really should read material that contains more than cartoons and colouring pages.'

James: 'Don't worry, I read Harvard, AFR and subscribe to a bunch of sales blogs... I know the latest trends in selling, LinkedIn, ROI analysis, client personality styles...remember that offsite with the weird facilitator in the orange socks that kept categorising us as blue sheep or green dogs or something? He suggested pigeon-holing all of our clients as if they were one dimensional...then we all got pissed.'

Sophie: 'I remember the bar bill very well, even today. We're meeting Mr. Selfin Terest, Intergalactic Head of Global Infrastructure and Resources.'

James: 'Wow....the   big   cheese....Selfin?   Isn't   he Scandinavian or Belgian or something?'

Sophie: 'Dutch.'

James: 'Well, as Nigel Powers famously said 'There's only two things I hate. People who are intolerant of other people's cultures and the Dutch.'

Sophie: 'Concentrate, will you? Selfin has your proposal and he has agreed to discuss it with us now.'

Level 31 (After pleasantries and stale water is served)

Selfin: 'Let me be really honest with you…when we first came to see you, we asked for a solution that was innovative and cost effective that gave us an edge over our competitors.

Frankly, whilst the ideas you've put forward have lots of potential, we can't see the payoff for at least three years.'

James: 'Yes, that's the ROI we discussed at the start, based on justifying the investment and….'

Sophie: 'Let Mr. Terest finish please, James.'

Selfin: 'We've chosen a less expensive solution that doesn't have all the bells and whistles but certainly plugs a hole for the next 12 months. Rest assured, we're happy to revisit it then and thanks so much for all your time and effort… I'm sure it won't be wasted for other bids you have.'

Back in the coffee shop

James: 'I don't get it. We put months into this, it covered their projected growth over three years and gave them a chance to get ahead of their competitors.'

Sophie: ' Yes, James, but there's one thing you didn't uncover: Selfin is moving back to the Netherlands next month and he doesn't believe his team here is capable of such a transition, regardless of the merits of the solution. The last thing he wants is to be jumping on planes to sort out a new implementation that he is still accountable for in his global role out of Amsterdam,'

James: 'How the hell do you know all that?'

Sophie: 'While you were working on the proposal I was working on Selfin and questioning his every move, pattern of decision making, career objectives and immediate goals. That's how I found out about his family's decision to move. We both know how underqualified his team are, so I knew we were dead in the water with our so-called innovative solution. I didn't tell you because I wanted you to go through it yourself…and besides, I've sandbagged another deal for you anyway.'

James: 'Bloody Selfin Terest.'

Sophie: 'Exactly, James – the greatest decision maker of all time.'

James: 'Thanks Sophie. Anyway, the good news is there's a PokeStop at this café and I think there's a Pikachu nearby.'

III

HOW TO AVOID LOSING

Why You Shouldn't Lose

9. DO YOU WANT A PROPOSAL WITH THAT ?

'Unsolicited advice is the junk mail of life.'

- Bern Williams

There are three certainties in life: Death, taxes and a manager asking if you've sent the client a proposal yet.

This unsolicited proposal behaviour is getting worse, not better, with many CRM systems requiring a tick in the box for a sent proposal before it recalibrates the magic opportunity management machine.

There are two massive opportunities to differentiate, save time and give the client what they really want to make decisions.

1. Stop Offering to Send a Proposal

You're on the last dregs of your coffee in a meeting with a potential client and the words come out of your mouth like a boring politician 'on message.'

'How about I send you a proposal?'

'Sure...' says the client. After all, it's not going to require any work on his/her part and it can be deleted faster than Snapchat if it's not interesting.

So, there you are at 7 pm in the office, your boss proudly looking at how hard you're working.

You've made the perfunctory call to your spouse to say you'll be a little late and spoken to the one kid who's there or awake about how tunnel ball was fun or how the maths teacher was too strict.

Then you get back to your 'unsolicited proposal.' What's in it?

Mostly, there isn't enough diagnosis of the client's real needs established so you default to a mix of your company overview and the fact you have $40 billion behind you and a global presence (or at least an office in Perth).

You add five heaped tablespoons of product, a teaspoon of services, a very mild seasoning of the perceived client's issues together with a dash of testimonials and a pinch of estimated pricing/fees.

It's about as tailored and well-fitting as a $99 suit....in microfibre.

It's taken you three hours to do two or three of these, you're tired and you've got 129 emails still banked up. But your CRM box is ticked!

The client receives this wishy washy effluent and reads a quarter of it if you're lucky, and then the tedious game of 'Did you get the proposal?' begins.

It's worse than watching 'Family Feud.'

If you're doing any of this, please 'STOP IT.' Go home. Have dinner with a client or, radically, even your spouse if they're still talking to you.

NEVER ask if they would like a proposal.

If they want one they'll ask for it, at which point please say 'Sure, what would you most like to see in it?'

If you really want to send them something, have a tight 5 slide/page credibility document that you can send in 1.4 seconds and set their expectations for what it is.

2. Only Ever Write Customised Proposals Written in the Client's Language

If the client asks for a proposal and you've double checked what they want, by all means spend a bit of time and ensure:

- The Executive Summary is about what's in it for them, not you.
- Your biggest, fattest testimonials or logos take up a whole page.
- The language is about their people, their processes, their challenges.
- The pricing is clear and has options.
- Use of images of their plant, equipment, locations, maps.
- You deliver it in person or over video conference (based on the size of deal you nominate).

Alternatively, they may just want a one pager or a simple quote. Yes, really.

Unlike McDonalds' profit enhancing Fries Question, asking the client if they want a proposal simply wastes your time, possibly theirs and potentially your family's.

If CRM and Sales Manager pain persists, see a doctor... or call me.

I'm unlikely to send you a proposal.

10. SERIAL SALES KILLER

'If you can meet with triumph and disaster and treat those two impostors just the same.'

- Rudyard Kipling

Are you strong enough to look deep into your own sales attitudes and behaviours?

Underneath the BMW/Audi, the tailored suit and the $200 haircut lies the dormant sales serial killer, potent enough to kill deals without leaving a trace of DNA.

No CSI team, deal post mortem or client de-brief could uncover the real murderer of highly profitable, high value wins.

The killer is called Attribution Bias...let's call him/her AB.....it's kind of catchy.

AB loves to take credit for a win and believes wholeheartedly that if it wasn't for h3im/her this bloody company would have ended up in the toilet a long time ago.

In fact, why there isn't a statue of them at reception is a complete mystery.

Equally AB loves to blame everybody else when a deal goes sour and again, if it wasn't for them they wouldn't have been that close in the first place.

You could at least say thank you for their efforts - it's not their fault the deal was lost.

AB essentially is biased in that too much credit is claimed for success and not enough responsibility is taken for failure.

Here are some examples of AB behaviour:

'The client's a dickhead - he doesn't even understand the technology.'

'I'm on my own here - the pre-sales resources are never there when you need them.'

'Why can't the global office understand that we can't charge that rate here?'

'It's only my relationship with this client that keeps this account alive.'

'It's unbelievable how long it takes to get a proposal done around here.'

'My boss is a dickhead.'

'The CRM is stuffed.'

'Nobody could sell that bundle of solutions into government/corporate/SMB without discounting.'

'My channel partner is a dickhead.'

'I always sell this way - if the client doesn't get it, I move on.'

'I absolutely need to take the client through my entire presentation/methodology, because I've seen it work before.'

'I was the Global Top Sales Achiever in 2009. This place doesn't get it.'

'My clients love me...that's why we win.'

'The marketing guy is a dickhead.'

These biases often prevent people from seeing things at their purest.

The reality is often different from your perception.

Some clients will buy from you and your company and some won't for all sorts of weird and wonderful reasons, but needing approval and validation from clients or shifting blame are not the best building blocks to long term success.

AB loses deals because opportunities are killed off as soon as the bias kicks in.

If you stop judging clients and the people around you and simply listen with empathy, observing the situation at hand from all angles, you are much better placed to uncover new opportunities, remove blocks, dissolve frustration and find new strategies to win business.

As paradoxical as it may seem, putting yourself at the centre of the deal is attributing far too much bias to the reality that is taking place around you.

Step back and see things for what they are, not what AB is telling you they are. Make choices.

That is ultimate empowerment.

When you lock AB away in a cell and throw away the key, then you can be released to be even more successful.

11. YOUR OWN WORST ENEMY

'Easy like Sunday morning.'

- Faith No More

Recently, I met with Don Peppers, recognised by Accenture in their Global Top 100 Business Intellectuals and by Satmetrix as the world's #1 most influential authority on customer experience management.

He has great insights into how to make it easy for people to buy, and coined 'the frictionless customer experience.'

We've all got our favourite stories about our less than helpful engagements as consumers of airlines, retail stores, food, insurance and Telcos.

The inflexible arsehole, the 'that's our policy' robot and the 'we don't serve chips with that' poncy chef.

In our world of B2B sales, many companies are their own worst enemy when it comes to making it easy to buy. You would think with millions of dollars at stake, people would ease the way faster than a lubricant demonstration at Sexpo.

Instead, this is dished up to clients:

- 'You want to see a demonstration next week– er, sorry, it takes us two weeks to get sign off from three living great-grandparents just to get access to the system.'

- 'We can't confirm the team who would be looking after your account until we sign the contract.'

- 'We couldn't give you even indicative pricing unless you fill in 72 specification sheets, provide us with exact numbers, locations and the "Who Do You Think You Are" ancestral history of all of your key stakeholders.'

- 'You really should meet our pre-pre-sales specialist, thirteen managers, our regional manager, our co-founder and our current acting CEO before we move to the next stage.'

- 'It would be good if you could sign a Letter of Intent because I'm not sure we'd have the stock in time otherwise.'

- 'Our legal representatives at Dewey, Farrkew and Howe have found a word they don't like on page 779 of the contract, which may be a problem.'

- 'Yes, the assumptions we've made are as long as the US Presidential Primaries and we may need to re-negotiate if you haven't disclosed everything including things you don't know.'

- 'I know you asked for left-handed widgets to be delivered on Wednesdays but we'd prefer it if you bought right-handed widgets on Fridays…in advance.'

- 'We need to have another 2 day workshop plus a needs analysis session, a full scale audit and a four hour site visit before we give you a full proposal.'

- 'I know we gave your procurement team a non-compliant response, but we wanted to shift your thinking and show how we do it.'

We get annoyed if our favourite hotel delivers the wrong newspaper or won't make a mushroom omelette the way we like it. We get irritated when you need an actuarial degree to decipher a mobile phone plan, and yet the same or far worse is perpetrated against corporate clients.

Find ways to say 'Yes.'

Listen to how the client wants to do things – you'd be surprised how often their preferences are not really going to make a huge difference to the material outcome.

Look at every step of the sale and ask 'How can this be made easy like Sunday morning?'

I know it sounds funny but I just can't stand the pain.

12. SALES GHOST STORIES THAT WIPE OUT WINNING

'Yesterday, upon the stair,
I met a man who wasn't there.
He wasn't there again today,
I wish, I wish he'd go away…'

- Hughes Mearns circa 1899

In selling, often we think and see things that simply aren't there. They are figments of our imagination based on fear of losing, low confidence or false perception – sales ghost stories!

Here are my top three ghost stories rolling around in the castle of our sales heads that can wipe out our chances of winning.

'I'm not sure our solution will work.'

This is one of the most common ghost stories out there because it's your reputation on the line and you are wary of burning relationships.

However, most organisations provide products and solutions that work, just not 100% of the time. They're not perfect, get over it.

You're probably reading this on a device that has crashed, spontaneously rebooted, not charged properly or failed to connect to the internet numerous times. (Usually when your forecast is due in half an hour.)

I'll bet you still use and even rave about your technology and can't wait to buy the next unproven piece of plastic from your favourite brand.

Bill Gates is still pretty rich, even after spending gazillions on helping to eradicate malaria. Windows and/or your hard drive never crashed on you, did it, causing you to lose your entire MBA thesis overnight? Yeah right! Yet the product was still sold and at its core the stuff works.

Ghost stories we tell ourselves that block our ability to freely discuss solutions and open up deals include:

- 'Pete in Pre-sales just resigned – there's no-one to do my demo so I'll wait until the new guy arrives.'

- 'The showroom/lab/office doesn't have Widget X so I can't invite the prospect in yet.'

- 'I heard a rumour from the receptionist who spoke to the Queensland Service Technician that Jane's client in Townsville complained that our system didn't have feature XB42 and they're really unhappy. Best to hold off with my new client for a bit then.'

- 'I didn't get an email back from Global Support about our new solution, so I'm certainly not going to meet with the client again until I do.'

Sure…keep waiting while your competition is acting, selling their imperfect solutions.

If it's not a ghost story and you genuinely think you've got a dud, ask your sales manager or MD.

If they say 'Hold off for a bit' then fine. Otherwise don't let anything stop you from exploring ideas with clients.

'The Client is King and I am just a humble servant.'

If you believe you are not at least a peer of the client in the solutions you provide, regardless of their title, you will not ask deep questions, challenge thinking or boldly jump up at the whiteboard to share insights.

The client goes to the toilet the same way you do (well, they might scrunch or fold differently), but like you, they have kids, stress and the same politics at work.

They have enough sycophants in the office sucking up to them, so they don't need you being all humble, seeking permission for every comment or overly using reflective questions to check back that they're happy with how the call is progressing.

All they want is for you to sit there as an equal, have a direct open business conversation about their needs and cut the overly polite, overly respectful 'Thank you so much', 'Would it be all right if…' and 'Oooh, you are so important' language.

'I make more money selling Widget X   rather than Product Y, so I want to steer the client that way.'

There's nothing like self-interest to cut off deals at the start.

Yes, by an anomaly of the flawed commission scheme you can make more money NOW by promoting one product or service over another.

The problem is a chunk of clients don't want to be steered to your proposal that is based more on how you can buy that new Audi or take your spouse to the Maldives for a week to see if they still like having sex.

The client will pick up any bias you have –they're not stupid and will feel you're not listening, not engaging and not interested in their needs when you keep coming back to your favourite money-making scheme.

So for every client that does go for it many others will switch off, which ultimately leaves you out of a deal and out of pocket.

Exorcise the ghosts rattling around in your head. If you do, the really spooky thing is you will win more business.

13. TOP 10 THINGS PRE-SALES AND EXPERTS DO THAT KILL DEALS

'Never become so much of an expert that you stop gaining expertise.'

- Denis Waitley

Pre-sales, gurus, solution architects, subject matter experts, wizards or whatever you call them in your organization, they are critical to winning complex deals.

Many a holiday house has been purchased by a sales person off the back of a guru who wowed the client with their consummate mind-boggling expertise.

If you have one, anoint their feet with ylang ylang oil and buy them the complete series of 'Breaking Bad' just to show you care.

However, there are other pre-sales experts who, despite their best intentions, cause more pain for clients and in fact actually lead the client to say:

'Nope…too hard, I'm going with someone else.'

Here are my top ten things pre-sales and experts do that can kill the deal.

1. Telling clients everything you've ever learned since you finished University

We know you have more letters after your name than a fake Nigerian Prince with an inheritance to share, but the client doesn't need to hear every teensy weensy detail of the origin of the technology, financial instrument or manufacturing process.

You may think it demonstrates expertise. It doesn't. It demonstrates you're as boring as listening to their Uncle Bert's incessant medical complaints.

Filter the content and only discuss the stuff that is highly relevant to them.

2. It's not a Debating Club

You may not agree with the client's views, but it's not an opportunity to stand there proudly rebutting the finer points because you may be technically correct to three decimal places on software revision 3.0115.

If the thing won't actually work, then you can succinctly guide the client to that fact. But nit-picking, pedantic points and correcting small errors on behalf of the client just pisses them off.

3. 'No, Nyet, Nup. Forget it. Can't be done.'

Really? The client seems keen on exploring a few options on how they might solve a problem only to be met with multiple forms of 'No.'

You might think that there's only one best way to do things because you've tested it in the lab or for another client, but there are almost always more ways to address issues than you first thought.

'I'm not sure yet, let's look into it a little further' is much more likely to keep the client engaged than a flat 'No, that can't be done.'

4. 'Let me tell you everything that could possibly go wrong.'

We know you have to cover your butt and set expectations, but telling the client you can't guarantee the solution if the wind's blowing the wrong way on a Wednesday, or if they miss a deadline by a minute, or they don't complete their side of things in time, or if there's a nuclear explosion within 200 kilometres, subject to Wireless working, which it often isn't, plus all their people need to be trained and accredited, blah, blah.

I feel like self-harming just writing this.

It's not helping the client; it's scaring the hell out of them.

5. 'Let's show you a 4 hour demonstration.'

'Come into our office and we'll make you feel like you've just watched *Titanic* twice back to back including the Celine Dion soundtrack on repeat loop.'

If you need hours to demonstrate your widgets, you don't understand the client well enough.

Try more discussion, enquiry and research and less actual demonstration. It is possible to show how things work in minutes, not hours.

6. Contradicting a colleague

We know you don't want the client to get the wrong advice, but when you blatantly say something like' Bob, I don't think what you've said is quite right' you become the married couple at the dinner table that everyone talks about afterwards, taking bets on how long before the divorce lawyers buy new Ferraris.

It screams no teamwork, no cohesion, no chemistry and no deal.

If Bob is wrong, take him aside during a break or afterwards and let him correct the situation.

7. 'If I were you, I'd buy Solution X.'

The problem is you're not them. Clients have different prejudices, politics, budgets, perceptions and agendas.

Just because you think it's great doesn't mean it fits the client's way of doing things.

If that was the case, 99% your clients would have Solution X, but they don't, do they? Bigotry is death to many deals.

8. Mitigated language

This is the first cousin of 'Can't be Done.'

Phrases like 'hopefully', 'possibly', 'perhaps', 'maybe', 'might', 'potentially', 'all things being equal' and 'in the long run' fill the audience with as much comfort as sitting next to the smelly fat guy on QF 464 to Sydney.

Quite simply, will your solution do the things you say and deliver the results you're promoting or not?

9. Interrupting

Knock, knock

Who's there?

Interrupting cow

Interrupting cow wh….MOOO!

Nobody likes to be interrupted…ever…under any circumstances. The client is sharing their story and you get excited about an area that's right in your sweet spot.

You've just interrupted them in full swing, so they stop telling you all that juicy stuff about their business and for what?

You then proudly share your rich knowledge which they might appreciate, but you've only learned half the story, assumed the rest, and now the momentum is lost. Don't Moo!

10. Staying too long

There is always someone at the party who outstays their welcome. You've subtly put on your dressing gowns, yawned five times, talked about going to bed and they are still sitting in your lounge room, drinking your Johnnie Walker Blue Label.

Clients want you to visit for a while too, share your expertise, explore alternatives and see what you've got, and then they have better things to do.

Get to the point, and then get out of there. Windbags aren't invited back.

Experts who communicate professionally are always welcome.

14. TOP 10 CRAPPY SALES BEHAVIOURS THAT ARE RUINING YOUR C-LEVEL MEETINGS

'Isn't it nice to think that tomorrow is a new day with no mistakes in it yet?'

- L.M. Montgomery

Do you remember how exciting it was to move up a grade in basketball, cricket, netball, football, karate or whatever your favourite sport was?

Do you also remember coming home after realising that your famed layup, defence, pace, inswinger, cut shot or height wasn't anywhere near as effective and that the other teams had you worked out pretty quickly?

C-Level Execs will also work you out in a matter of 7 minutes as to whether you are a good old fashioned slogger in a suit or a legitimate source of trust, advice and opportunity.

Here are the top ten crappy sales behaviours that can ruin your C-Level Meetings.

1. 'Thanks very much for your time, I know you're a busy person and appreciate you agreeing to see me.'

Aaaargh..! In the first 30 seconds you've just said 'Hello O Great One, I am but a humble seller trading my wares.' It's not polite and respectful. It screams 'I am not an equal and don't treat me like one.' What's wrong with 'Good to meet you'?

2. Fake rapport

Yes…you've done it – chatted inanely about the weather, his lovely office, last night's football match, recent election results or other vomitous topics. It seemed reasonable with the mid-level manager who had football posters on his wall, but all the C-Level Exec wants is authenticity, not some cheap speed dating repartee. Try mentioning what you've learned of his industry, not the picture of the marlin on the wall.

3. Bunny Boiler

You're 5-10 minutes into a meeting and you start talking about how you're a company that's looking for a relationship, a partnership. If that was you on a date you'd secretly pull a nostril hair, fake a nose bleed and get out of there faster than you can say Glenn Close. You don't even know what s/he wants in the C Suite. It might be a quick win or it might be strategic, so relax about the long term relationship stuff until you know each other a little better.

4. Prescriptive agendas

If you went out with a friend and upon arriving at the restaurant, your mate said 'So, first I think we should talk about your job, then I'll discuss my promotion, then it would good to hear about your ex-wife and finally we'll wrap up with any questions', what would you do? You'd say 'Are you completely nuts, what's wrong with you?'

The C-Level Decision Maker doesn't want you to drive him/her through a prescriptive agenda. They want you to have a business conversation that is free flowing and explores all sorts of interesting ideas and issues in the business.

5. Crapping on

There's a time in most meetings when you have an opportunity to discuss your products/services, but make it short, valuable and relatable. If you're still banging on after 5 minutes about your wonderfully unique, exciting, holistic, integrated end to end solution, you've become the self indulgent talking to the self interested. Not conducive to a longer meeting.

6. Listening only to the bits that interest you

Your C-Level friend is exploring a number of concerns but it's 20 minutes in and you're worried that none of their issues seem to relate to your widgets. Panic sets in and you abruptly steer the conversation like an L Plater on a freeway into a topic more amenable to discussing your favourite solutions.

Clunk! You've just cut them off in a major lane change and you know how much you love that on the highway. They hate it too.

7. Whipping it out

Out comes the iPad, PowerPoint Presentation, Prezi, booklet, brochure or whatever crappy material Marketing gave you that quarter. No matter how skilfully it's done, it all looks like 'Here's one we prepared earlier.' Untailored stodge. If you need to be visual, use a whiteboard on the fly.

8. No flag of hope

In the late, great Robin Williams' infamous dissertation on the invention of golf, he describes the use of the green as 'At the end we'll put a flat piece with a flag to give you f*king hope.'

C-Level People want hope too. They are hoping that you are not a time-wasting tosser that is going to lead them down the garden path with no proven experience of success.

Tell them stories of successes in their industry. Make sure they know there are wins to be had in engaging you, rather than possible maybes after we've plugged some numbers into a spreadsheet.

9. Shoving yourself down the food chain

You've worked hard to get to C-Level. You and your company have earned the right to be there. Great! So please don't find yourself asking to be shunted down the chain of command with comments like 'Would it possible to meet with the IT/Finance/Operations Manager' because they'll more than likely say yes. It's now off their plate and they're thinking if the ideas are any good they'll re-surface in 3 months' time back up the line after you've worked your butt off trying to win over multiple stakeholders. If the ideas don't pop back up on their radar, they were probably not strong enough anyway.

It's much more effective upon the flicker of interest to say 'OK, how about you and I schedule another meeting to discuss this further. How would you recommend WE engage the rest of the business?' Peer-to-peer. The Power of We.

10. Sales 101

Sales 101 said you should actually do some of the above. Sales 101 said you should control the meeting. Sales 101 said you should ask leading questions to get the client to see your value proposition. To paraphrase Monty Python, Sales 101 is not resting, it's dead, it has ceased to be, it is an ex-methodology, it's expired, shuttled off this mortal coil and gone to meet its maker.

15. WHY DO CLIENTS CHEAT ON YOU?

'Busy is a drug that a lot of people are addicted to' – Rob Bell

Tales of infidelity have been splashed across the news everywhere for years. Clinton, Schwarzenegger, Spitzer as well as Kristen Stewart and Tiger Woods. There's even a TV show called 'Cheaters' salaciously exposing the lame offender for all to see.

Everyone has different reasons for cheating but Ruth Houston; a New York infidelity expert has distilled the main causes into a few key points.

These reasons have a direct correlation to the issue many companies face of 'Why did my client cheat on me with a competitor?' It's that sinking feeling you dread when you and your sales manager walk into your existing client's reception area to find opposition products sitting neatly on a pallet next to the replacement filtered water bottles.

It's the stomach churn when you sign into the visitor's book at reception and you see your competitor's name just above yours, having just been there four hours earlier to see your key contact.

Let's examine some of Ms. Houston's reasons for cheating and see how we can keep our clients monogamous.

Note: Please replace sex with 'value'. This is a business book and we are talking about client relationships, not the ones that involve dodgy text messaging and hotel rooms.

1. More sex.

Clients simply want more. You think you've given it your all in servicing their needs but they still want more value, bang for buck, faster delivery. We have to be really diligent in understanding that relationships are not static and what was once acceptable becomes unacceptable over time.

If you're in doubt about this one, look over to the next cubicle and ask one of your married (or divorced) colleagues!

2. Variety of sex

People get bored. Simple. You may think you're safe and reliable in that you've looked after your account for five years, but what have you done to freshen it up? Are there new ways of looking after their business; new ways of bundling services? Isn't it about time you mixed it up a bit – gave the clients a different subject matter expert or a new account manager with fresh eyes to liven it up?

3. You don't make me feel special any more

The expression 'taken for granted' is taken for granted. We all know we shouldn't be complacent or rely on email instead of face to face engagement, BUT is still happens far too frequently.

Clients know when you're going through the motions, you're not 'sending them flowers, surprising them with a new restaurant or giving them a metaphorical back rub'. They want to feel special – that's why they ask you seemingly innocuous questions like 'So what other clients have you won recently?' They are often really saying 'do you still love me?' Show it.

4. Sexual curiosity

Ruth Houston discusses mild infatuation or curiosity in depth. People are curious and interested in 'the other'. Despite the mantras of 'our clients love us or our clients would be crazy to leave us', many of them are looking around and they are often attracted to that cute new piece of software that their friends are talking about at the pub.

Clients want you to be innovative with your solutions – they have no reason to cheat if you are consistently making yourself more attractive and engaging them with new ideas.

Clients cheat for all sorts of reasons and it is disingenuous and far too simplistic to say it was price or that the system was down for too long.

The real reasons in our personal lives are often the same in our business lives.

I have to go now… this hotel room only books by the hour…..

16. SALE INTERRUPTED

Give yourself a tick for each one of these statements you've made in the past month:

'Mate, I'm absolutely flat chat at the moment'

'Sorry, I'm completely smashed for time right now'

'I'm busier than a mosquito at a honeymooners' nudist beach in a city that banned Citronella'

Of all the reasons why win rates don't improve for many companies, including the perennials of 'talking to the right level' and 'differentiated value propositions', the killer is sheer, unadulterated time and focus on the client you really want to win.

I wonder how polygamists manage their week. Must be exhausting, mentally and physically to keep up with 14 spouses, 35 kids and three documentary filmmakers!

You can juggle, multi-task, fast-track, shuffle or prestidigitate (Look it up) as much as you want but nothing improves win rates on big deals more than taking the proper time to strategise, design, create and tailor a journey and a pitch that makes the client say:

'Wow, these guys really, really understand everything about us and their solution fits like a glove'

But the interruptions seem endless – emails, forecasting, internal meetings, presentations, compliance meetings, coffees, more coffees, tenders, product updates, reviews, needy clients, needy staff, knee-deep in sh*t!

A habit is formed where a big deal is treated the same way as all the other deals except for a few more meetings – fast, cursory and lacking deep insight or creativity.

I'm more like Yogi Bear than an advocate of Yoga but breathe in, lift your left leg and consider saying the following:

'No, I'm working on the Fudsucker Poobah deal – go away'.

'I need everyone, the CEO, the Head of Product, the Technical Guru and the Bear Grylls Tender Response Team in a room for a day, not an hour'.

'Please put Jaxon and Zalika (there are no John and Janes any more) on our existing accounts while we focus on Mr Fudsucker and the other senior executives right now'.

'If it meant that our company would go under if we don't win this deal, what would we ALL do?'

Do it.

The most excruciating sound in the world is not nails on a chalkboard, a Vuvuzela or your spouse's snoring. It's this:

'Thanks for all your effort with this bid. Look, it was very close and frankly, we could've chosen either company, but unfortunately for you, we've decided to go with the other mob'.

IV

SECRETS TO WINNING

Real Stories on How to Win

17. GAME OF THROWNS

'Winter is Coming.'

As you finish your third soy chai, double shot, espresso macchiato latte, you look over your account plan, your presentation, probing guide and signed off pricing for your meeting with a client.

'All sorted' you whisper to yourself, filled with the pride of preparation.

You've allowed enough time to get through the horrendous traffic, pre-booked a car park and even allocated ten minutes to sign into that stupid iPad security system that doesn't yet have your new client's name registered.

You begin the meeting well, until 10 minutes in and the client throws a curve ball.

'I'm no longer looking after that area of the business.'

'I've now been told we have to go to tender.'

'This now won't happen this financial year.'

'Actually, my new boss, Stacy, has a good relationship with one of your competitors, so I don't know where it goes from here.'

'I know we said we'd go ahead in June, but we now want you to do a full proof of concept and visit sixteen sites in rural

Australia on a Malvern Star bicycle wearing only your underpants and a flowerpot on your head.'

We are now in a game of being thrown.

In my research, role plays and in pitch consulting, only 30-40% of sales people ask 'Why?'

The majority, thrown off track, start mumbling like Sylvester Stallone with a mouthful of pastrami, almost pleading for guidance with the next step.

'Could you please introduce me to Stacy/Procurement/The Weird Proof of Concept Guy?'

or

'Ok, that's a shame…well let me know when you're ready then.'

'or

'As soon as I leave here I'll be getting a new pair of Bonds, pumping up the bicycle and going straight to the flowerpot shop.'

The key question is what do you want to do?

If the answer is acquiesce, go ahead and you can stop reading this and get your fourth coffee for the day.

Here are some options as to what you can do.

- Always ask 'Why?' Put it back on the client. Let them fully explain why circumstances have changed. After they've told you, you may want to ask 'Why?' again until you clearly understand all the politics, financials and timing issues.

- Don't ask permission to do what you need to do. If you need to now get to Stacy, just do it or do it in conjunction with your manager.

- If it's financials and you've just spent 6 months proving your case just to be told it's shut down, connect with the CFO, share your evidence and ask why.

- Don't just run around the country for free in the hope of 'staying in the game.' Look at rebateable fees for consulting or getting a commitment up front based on the proof of concept working.

- Discuss the advantages and disadvantages of going to tender with Procurement. Believe it or not there are some professional procurement people out there who are open to solving supply chain issues whilst retaining competitive tension without going to tender.

We are prone to being thrown. We get anxious when we don't get a text back in 0.3 nanoseconds or if we haven't heard from a client.

'They said they'd get back to us on Wednesday, OMG…it's now Thursday…they must not want us anymore.'

We get thrown when our inner control freak freaks out.

Yet the unexpected, the transitory, the delayed, the uncertain is the norm.

You can't control it.

What you can control is your reaction…and in this Game of Throwns you should not be exposed to nudity and your deal should not be killed.

18. WHY YOUR PITCH NEEDS A COLONOSCOPY

"A colonoscopy is like a video camera on the end of a Roto-Rooter.'

- Robin Williams

Bend down before you get bent over.

The two most common forms of assessing sales performance are before and after the deal.

Before the deal, there are forecasting meetings, commit meetings and hasty appraisals of a deal's winnability, because everyone is flat chat and a number needs to go in by midnight to keep someone happy somewhere in the world of sales operations.

After the deal, if it's a win - great.

If it's a loss there's public lynching, more finger pointing than a football referee, often followed by the same lame attempts at retrieval as those of a 3 legged cocker spaniel with a bent stick.

Confronting the effectiveness of the deal strategy is often not done well and pitch/presentations/client meetings go ahead with half-baked and often untested value propositions.

It's time to get comfortable with the rubber glove.

Professional sales teams book in pitch colonoscopies to have their deals probed, picked apart, differentiated and made compelling BEFORE they hit the client's eyes and ears.

People still believe in hope, the tooth fairy and their existing so-called fabulous relationships to win.

Key questions that should be asked are:

'Why should this client at this particular time see this as important?'

'Why are you not just capable, but absolutely differentiated as best fit?'

'What do your client's most senior executives know or think about you?'

'What are you presenting that is going to WOW them?'

'What have you done to accommodate the egos, politics and personalities of each decision maker?'

There are at least twenty others that discover polyps, cysts and other brown sticky stuff that prevent pitches from telling a genuinely persuasive story.

One of the best organisations I've seen is a top tier professional services firm that spent 3 days, including senior partner time at gazillions of dollars an hour, testing their colleagues' pitch.

The ramifications were significant in that 110 jobs were at risk if they didn't hold on to that account.

During one of my sessions with them I asked the managing partner 'How did you develop such a professional, robust culture of critique, confrontation and analysis to win major accounts?'

He said 'Do you know how much it costs to recruit and train 110 people - we're not losing this on my watch.'

In a time of political correctness (the definition of which is that it presupposes you can pick up a turd from the clean end), sensitivity and ego management, too many problems with deals are not picked up and confronted early enough.

Issues are glossed over or forgotten, not enough time is dedicated to strategy and too much undifferentiated drivel is pitched to clients, affecting win rates.

It can be uncomfortable bending down and having your deal exposed.

It's more devastating to waste months on a lost deal that could have been won.

Next time, get a team comprised of your CFO, CTO, Director or head of a different product division to listen to your deal, watch your pitch and pick it to pieces.

It may be the best use of internal resources you make all year.

Alternatively, call me. I have warm hands.

19. TOP 5 WAYS TO REALLY SHORTEN SALES CYCLES

'Opportunities are like sunrises. If you wait too long, you miss them.' — *William Arthur Ward*

According to Qvidian research, only 63% of sales people will make their sales target.

That leaves over a third of you either auditioning in the tap section of 'So You Think You Can Dance' with your manager or connecting with a dozen more recruiters on LinkedIn.

If you managed to reach or exceed quota…well done; but it was probably harder than ever and one of the key culprits is the 'Long Sales Cycle' -the Golden Staph of Selling.

Here are my Top Five Ways to Shorten Sales Cycles.

Stop talking to the flunky

Your main mid-level contacts have limited budgets and authority.

They don't know everything that's going on in their organisation.

When they say 'I have no budget for 12 months' it's probably true and simply an inconvenient fact.

Your mother didn't even carry you in the womb for that long, so why gestate him for 12 months in a long sales cycle?

Start talking to C-Level and get your whole organisation involved. They will be able to move faster than a politician at a baby photo shoot if your solutions can help their business.

Twelve months becomes three if the right executive hears your potent story.

Use the client's balance sheet

One company went back to their client and asked how the financial return or ROI was faring on their implemented solution.

The client smiled like a kid who got away with farting in Science class and said 'Oh, we virtually paid for it in 6 weeks.'

The sales manager said '6 weeks! Fantastic, but why did you bash us around for weeks for reduced pricing if you knew the ROI was that good'?

The client smiled again (must be an on-going flatulence problem) and said 'Just part of the game – we knew we could delay and push you against your quarterly targets….bit of fun, really.'

Find someone who can read a proper balance sheet, a director, your CFO or your Weird Uncle Archie who likes Over 50s Singles Ballroom Dancing but also happens to be a qualified CPA.

Nothing shortens the sales cycle more than when you walk in with financial proof that every month they delay is costing them money or poor Return on Assets/Capital/Cash Flow.

Qualify like a reality TV show

If you've watched any of the talent shows on TV, you know they are ruthless in weeding out the people who can't cook, sing, dance or walk a catwalk.

They even flaunt it for their own glory by showing you brief shots of these insecure, destroyed souls who missed out on the chance to burn a soufflé on national television.

Anyone who has been to an audition knows that it's more ruthless than an FBI investigation.

Despite Bid/No Bid Systems, Sales Meetings and Forecasts, qualification is still done poorly.

Mostly, it's because the pipeline isn't big enough so we hang on to prospects more than we keep our favourite pair of worn, de-elasticised, comfy undies.

Yes, the red ones.

Poor qualification leads to long sales cycles and forecasts about as accurate as the Bureau of Meteorology -the place where pathological liars are sent for work experience.

Let's have the courage to ask prospects questions like:

'Based on our initial meeting/s, before we go any further, the budget for this is typically around 300-500k. Are you happy to continue talking?'

'We have three experts coming off projects in June who will then be allocated for the next major client assignment.'

'What are your thoughts on that timeframe for you?'

If the answers are positive, you've shortened the sales cycle. If not, you can still keep them warm, but they're not part of a long sales cycle because they have qualified themselves out.

Your hairdresser, masseur or car mechanic does this effortlessly.

There's no need to be squeamish about 'Are you ready for us or not?'

As the great philosopher Beyoncé said ,'If you liked it then you should have put a ring on it.'

Stop being the clingy, needy boyfriend/girlfriend. Move or move on.

Get your really senior management involved

In my work consulting on major pitches, I have seen tremendous results by getting your CEO, Regional Director, Global CEO or Chief Superintendent of Intergalactic Greatness to call the client.

Depending on the situation, he or she may say one of the following things to your client's senior management:

'My people have been working with your people for 6 months – this has global visibility at our end and the ROI seems to be less than 12 months.'

'What's the hold up?' or 'What hasn't my team done to prove this yet?'

'I've just come back from a meeting with one of your competitors who implemented our solution months ago.'

'Help me understand why this appears to be dragging on so long.'

'With respect, I can't give you our global expert, Rita, any further without some understanding of where this is going and when it will move forward.'

Basically, it's the Jerry Maguire moment; 'Show Me The Money.'

Timeline on a whiteboard

We have used this to help win pitches for years.

NOW _____THEN

You work backwards from 'THEN', the point in time where they indicate they need to see a result in cost reduction, implementation, cash flow improvement, customer acquisition or whatever their Holy Grail is.

You then fill in the blanks with:

- 6 weeks to implement and train

- 5 weeks for testing

- 7 weeks for Procurement and shipping

- 2 weeks for business analytics

- 4 weeks for stakeholder engagement and signoff, etc. etc.

Before you know it, it will often become evident that they should have ordered this thing in 1978 to get the results they want.

Too many sales people do the opposite by promising that they'll expedite things to help.

All that does is take the pressure off the client to commit because s/he knows you'll run around like a Coke addict (not the Cola kind) to get things done, even if they delay the decision making.

Stuff that for a game of Monopoly.

Show them the real timeline that has built-in protection, assurance and quality and ask them if they want to get a 457

Visa for Dr Who to time travel back to meet the deadlines or simply place the PO now.

Shortening sales cycles is like sticking to the speed limit to avoid penalties. You have more control than you think.

20. TOP 10 ONE LINE MYTHS ABOUT SELLING

'Don't be satisfied with stories; how things have gone with others. Unfold your own myth.'

- Rumi

In honour of David Letterman's 33 years, here are my Top Ten One Line Myths About Selling:

1. 'It's a numbers game.' Not if your volume is based on calling the equivalent of your Aunt Maureen.

2. 'Clients are your friends.' Nope. Your friends are the ones that love you despite knowing that weird s**t you pulled off in Year 12.

3. 'Selling is about asking questions.' Not if they mostly relate to you and your product.

4. 'Sex sells.' If you want to time travel back to 1980 maybe.

5. 'Negotiation is win-win.' Actually, it's OK if one side gets more. It doesn't need to be fair, just good business.

6. 'Clients spend a lot of time analysing you and your company.' Not as much as their real work, Facebook, their kids and analysing their boss.

7. 'Mentioning other clients or competitors is unethical.' Not if it's indisputably true.

8. 'It's important to listen for buying signals/clues.' Does that mean you're not going to listen to the other so-called less relevant stuff the client is saying?

9. 'Sales cycles are getting longer.' Only if you allow it by not differentiating in the very first meeting at the right level.

10. 'Top 10 sales myth lists are too simplistic.'

21. SALIENT SALES LESSONS FROM YOUR FAVOURITE MOVIES

'It's funny how the colours of the real world only seem really real when you watch them on a screen.'

Anthony Burgess, A Clockwork Orange

The Shawshank Redemption

- You have to crawl through 500 yards of sh*t to come out clean at the other end.

- If you're planning a secret strategy, cover it up while you go about your everyday business. Don't tell everyone else about it, lest the warden find out.

- Understand financials: ROI, ROA, ROCE and learn how your client actually makes money and measures value.

A Few Good Men

- Don't blindly follow the rules if it breaches your personal values.

- The General can be probed (CIO, CEO, CFO) so you can understand his emotional triggers such as pride, ego, fear, or status.

- Seek and handle the truth, no matter what is thrown at you.

- Get the CEO to lead you right where you want him to go. Of course he ordered the Code Red Procurement Strategy. Deal with it.

Forrest Gump

- You don't have to have an IQ of 150 to be successful.

- Sometimes you just have to run and run with an idea and people will follow you.

- Try different things, don't over analyse, meet diverse people, listen to other people's ideas, and take action.

- Tell your story to lots of people.

Psycho

- Pretending to be someone else never works.

- It can be very isolating by yourself (see Branch Managers/Home Workers) and you get a very distorted view of the world without other people around.

- You can get into an awful lot of trouble harassing people in your workplace.

The Godfather

- When deciding your final proposal, make them an offer they can't refuse.

- Always consider the importance of succession planning and training when sales people and accounts get whacked.

- If you really hate what your competitor is doing, find a way to take them out (er. legally).

Titanic

- Going full speed ahead without observing what's going on around you can leave you blindsided.

- If you're embarking on a maiden voyage new sales approach, don't become arrogant about its success until you've reached the destination.

- If you're sinking, have enough resources to jump into a new strategy life boat.

Silence of the Lambs

- Get inside the client's head; master Hannibal's 'Tell Me' and 'Why' questions.

- 'Tell me about the lambs, Clarice.'

- 'Why do you think he removes their skins, Agent Starling?'

- 'Quid pro quo – I tell you things. You tell me things.'

James Bond

- Always look the part, even if you've had your head blown off by a competitor.

- Learn to use all the latest technology (social media, CRM, mobility).

- There is always a way of negotiating your way out of tricky situations.

- The bad guys always lose in the end.

22. I KNOW WE SHOULDN'T BUT IT'S END OF QUARTER

'Courage. Now that's the stuff leaders should be made of. Now I have come to the crossroads in my life. I always knew what the right path was. Without exception, I knew. But I never took it. You know why? It was too damn hard.'

- Al Pacino, Scent of a Woman.

Tick, tick, tick...You're a week away from end of quarter or financial year and the sphincter tightening is on full clench.

When first researching end of quarter behaviour, I posted a short LinkedIn question 'If you were selling your house on Sunday, you wouldn't just drop the price 20% because the buyer asked you to. So, why would you do it at work on Monday?'

The response from experienced professionals and sales leaders was unanimous: 'END OF QUARTER.'

Two weeks later I hosted a panel including CxOs, sales experts and sales leaders and discussed the same topic.

After a two day conference where everyone was filled with the joys of strategy, enthusiasm for coaching the right sales behaviours, consummate sales visions and case studies, the elephant in the room became an entire zoo when people were asked if they would stay the course if poor end of quarter figures were looming.

There was more shifting in seats than a flatulence convention followed by 'It depends', 'Ya still gotta get the number' and the wonderfully ambivalent analogy 'If I'm giving up smoking and I relapse by having one or two, then it doesn't mean I'm not still giving up smoking.'

Er...doesn't that 'relapse' matter if you're the leader that's been telling people to give up smoking for months?

Don't you love self righteous justifications?

So, let's look at the most common behaviours that take place at end of quarter and their impact.

'Mummy, I'm scared...'

'I forecasted X to Global and we're 22% down. Where's my magic discount calculator? That's right – hidden under that new Leadership book I bought at the airport. Hey...All hands on deck. Tell anyone who has ever spelled our company name correctly that they can have the same widgets for 20% less if they order by Wednesday.'

Begging

Please Mr Customer...I'll be your best friend, mow your lawn for a week and give you back rubs every Friday afternoon if you'll sign the PO in the next 2.4 seconds.

The hairdryer

Gathering up the sales team and delivering a blistering verbal attack on their appalling inability to do what you hired them to do.

The worst case of this was a CEO who came down near the end of December and called the entire sales team 'Two Star Parasites.' True story.

He then wished everyone Merry Christmas.

Financial fudgery

Playing jiggery- pokery with the system, quotas, inventory, invoices, commissions or whatever else will make it look good.

Whatever it takes

Got an indirect channel strategy? F*ck it, let's go direct. Agreed minimum margins become a polite suggestion. Start invading sales territories like a four year old on red cordial....straight from the bottle.

You might say 'Hey, this is the real world, mate, and it has to be done this way.'

At least consider the major impacts on your business:

  1. Train your clients to expect discounts quarterly and they will wait and salivate like Pavlov's Dog

dragging your revenue and margins down into the doggie bowl for a long time.

2. Beg your customer and in many cases you will lose trusted advisor status and commoditise yourself as 'just another supplier.'

3. Attack and blame the sales team and reflect on your staff retention numbers in 12 months' time when the head hunters find out.

4. Someone with a personality disorder who wears thick glasses and cardigans in Global Operations will find your fudgery eventually.

5. Break the rules, destroy the strategy and throw sales behavioural change out the window for expediency and watch a confused, dispirited bunch of people at the coffee shop talking incessantly about sales transformation not being taken seriously.

The real world is not perfect, and reasonable compromises that are extremely well communicated can still be made.

However, if you're serious about growth, client trust, and developing truly professional sales strategies and people, then it takes leadership.

As Warren Bennis famously said 'Managers do things right. Leaders do the right thing.'

Even at End of Quarter.

23. THE SCHMOOZE IS DEAD

'When you see the genuine, you don't deal with the fakes anymore.'

- Nima Davani

Popular business commentator Alan Kohler interviewed me on 'Pitching to Win' for Qantas Talking Business.

Here is the transcript:

Alan: Joining me now is Elliot Epstein, CEO of Salient Communication. Elliot is, well he's three things: Trainer, speaker and pitch consultant. Talk to me about pitch consulting, Elliot.

Elliot: Well Alan, it's really about those large multimillion dollar deals that people have from time to time. They might only be two or three a year that companies have in B2B selling but they're must win. If they don't win, people get sacked, divisions close down, things become dire. I get the phone call when it's high stakes and I work with them to develop that pitch, test it and give them winning themes that they haven't already thought of.

Alan: Big companies mostly should know what they're doing in this area. Why do they have to bring you in?

Elliot: That's a very good point because most organizations have internal resources, they have sales development programs, and they have sales academies from time to time so...

Alan: They have very well-paid sales people presumably...

Elliot: They do.

Alan   ...doing their PowerPoint presentations and stuff like that.

Elliot: Yes, we don't need more PowerPoint presentations.

Alan: What do you tell them?

Elliot: Basically I tell them the truth. They hire me to tell them the truth, and that involves testing because they get caught up drinking their own...

Alan: Big companies don't tell each other the truth, do they? It's true, I know that's true. People don't tell the truth to each other.

Elliot: Internally they believe their own BS and they believe their own stories so much that they think the client automatically gets it. All the internal marketing, all the internal conversations are about how good they are. They're pumping themselves up and they think the client just buys the traditional line. There was a case recently I worked on... a very, very large, highly contested deal where a very senior manager was flown in from overseas. No one would confront him.

Alan: To run the pitch.

Elliot: To run the pitch, to be the pitch leader and no one would confront him on the fact that what he was saying sounded great but the client wasn't buying it. The client had actually said to them, 'You're coming second. We still want to see what you're doing. We still want to move to the next phase but as it sits right, now you're behind.' They still wanted to go down the same path of promoting the same messages.

Alan: They weren't going to change their pitch?

Elliot: No, they just kept wanting to repeat it and come up with a different ROI.

Alan: What did you tell them? How did you shift them?

Elliot: I said, 'Do you want to win or not?'

Alan: Right, yes, the answer was yes.

Elliot: They said, 'Yes,' and I said, 'Let me tell you from 16 years of watching pitches what I'm hearing versus what you're saying and what the client might be hearing. Perhaps we might want to change that and hear some fresh ideas as to how you could present what you're talking about.'

Alan: Right, did they get it?

Elliot: Eventually... he looked at me and he said, 'Are we paying you?' I said, 'Apparently, I haven't sent an invoice yet.' He said, 'Well if we're paying you I better listen.'

Alan: How much were they paying you? Can you tell me that?

Elliot: I'm not going to tell you the numbers but it's not a percentage...

Alan: What do you charge generally?

Elliot: Typically you're looking at a pitch might be anywhere from $10,000 to $30,000 to work on a large deal depending on the scope. Then occasionally there're success fees if they win and obviously nothing if they lose. We've got a 79% hit rate over 12 years on multi-million dollar, highly contested deals, which is not bad considering you can't control the solution.

Alan: No indeed, and it's not your business in the sense that as you say you can't control them entirely. You can tell, you can give them advice, but like all consultants it's...

Elliot: It's up to them.

Alan: It's up to them.

Elliot: A few of the key themes that come out that might be interesting for people to note is that the client is interested in more than just the fact that you can provide the solution. That they've already chosen you as one of three in the shortlist. They've already been to your premises. They've Googled everything you've ever produced. They already know that you're capable, so wasting time proving capability is exactly that: a sheer waste of time. What they want is why you are absolutely clinically differentiated for them, not just in the marketplace. Don't show me charts of market leadership; show me why you are better for them, that particular client at this particular moment in history.

That's what people struggle with. They struggle with that final inch if you like, that final centimetre that says, 'Okay this is why we're better, not generically but very specifically across all of the client's needs as to how they're going to get a much, much better result, not just a marginally better result.'

Alan: To what extent does the pitch need to appeal to the individual who's the buyer as opposed to the company?

Elliot: That's critical and a lot of people do miss that, Alan. They think that it's all about the company outcome: Return on investment, total cost of ownership, all those buzzwords. Three letter acronyms that people get excited about are mostly rubbish because they're all interpreted by clients very differently. Individual representation and connection is critical. That means well, what are the egos in the room? Are we playing to the egos properly? Are we playing to the scaredy cats who've got a little puddle around the floor where they're considering what will happen if they don't get the right result from this solution? What do you do with the ambitious people in the room? Have you got something in there that's going to appeal to their sense of ambition and drive?

What about the greedy ones? How are you going to appeal to the greedy ones out there? And the ones that are sheer darn lazy? One of the things that happens in most large-scale deals is that there's transition involved. When you're transitioning that means it's almost like moving house: We all think it's a pain in the butt. No one really loves moving house. If you're moving one system out for one system in or one supplier out for another, there's a chunk of work there. There's a huge project to be involved in.

Alan: And who can be bothered.

Elliot: Yeah well, who can be stuffed doing that? The client, the pitchers who get that right sell transition as a very easy process rather than making it look hard. The ones that understand that you've got an ego-head on the other side of the desk simply make them look good every single time they engage rather than challenging them because it's supposedly the right thing to do. So, the individual is key.

Alan: How is B2B selling changing?

Elliot: Nowadays, there's a huge amount of change. There's probably more sales training development companies than I've ever seen in the 16 years I've been doing this. There are huge differences between what used to happen and what's happening now. Everyone's got a framework, everyone's got a methodology, everyone's got their favourite seven steps to glory. But the key difference today is that because there's more noise and because clients have far more access to information than they've ever had before, you've got to differentiate clearly. A lot of the sales training and development is still predicated on the supplier being better. The supplier demonstrating. The supplier challenging. The supplier doing something that is 'salesy'.

Alan: Which supplier? The supplier to you or you as a supplier?

Elliot: No, the vendors of solutions and systems. Those people have been told they've got to talk about their widget, still. They're still taught by people to pitch and present and use PowerPoint and whiteboards and whatever else to tell them how good ... tell people how good their stuff is. Well in a country like Australia especially, we have natural conversations in the pub, in the coffee shops with our families. We're not a formal culture and yet there's a formality that comes about from some of those that I call older methodologies that is not natural in its conversational style.

What I teach is how basically to take that style that you would have in a pub with a mate, to a C-level executive and engender a relationship that is far more beneficial for them. Once they see that you're natural and adding value along the way and being honest and transparent, then you're more likely to win larger scale deals.

Alan: I get the sense that in our days it was all about relationships. You went out on the weekends with the people and you tried to cultivate friendships with the clients, so-

Elliot: Yes that's right.

Alan: Is that gone now?

Elliot: It's pretty much gone. It's what I call 'The Schmooze is Dead.'

Alan: Yeah the Schmooze is dead, isn't it?

Elliot: Yes, primarily because if you look at the clients, you're looking at typically at C-level where I coach people to win business, 35-55 year-old probably what... 70%+ male? Most of them are either married or divorced with a couple of kids probably at school. What are they doing with their lives, these clients that you're pitching to? They don't want to spend time with you on a rubbish football match on Friday night. They've got wives, they've got husbands, they've got junior footy on the weekend with kids. They've got elderly parents potentially they're looking after. I'm going to spend time with me-

Alan: They're busy.

Elliot: They're busy. More busy than they've ever been. Look, in an existing account relationship sure, yeah there's few lunches and dinners. To win business the schmooze is dead.

Alan: There you have it folks, the schmooze is dead; I love it. I've been talking to Elliot Epstein, CEO of Salient Communication.

You can also listen to this interview at:

https://soundcloud.com/elliot-epstein-1/qantas-talking-business-elliot-epstein

24. PLANNING YOUR PITCH ON A PLANE

If you travel a lot, you've probably got a huge presentation to deliver an hour after you land. Your client, leadership team, regional executives or fellow industry experts expect you to be good. You had no time to fully prepare the whole presentation because it was chaos back at the office and there are still 292 unread emails sitting in your Inbox.

Now you have anywhere from 1-15 hours on a plane without interruption (except from the boring guy next to you with body odour like curdled milk who wants to sell you something).

Here are 5 ways you can maximise your time to be able to present like a star the minute you reach your destination.

1.   Edit like a film director.

I can't see your presentation from here but I'll bet it has too much information. Filmmakers typically cut from 8-10 hours of footage to get the final 2 hour edit you see at the cinema. Ask yourself one question "Why am I showing them this?" If you don't have an 8/10 reason, get rid of it. It will distil the focus to the content your audience really wants and keep them engaged.

2. **Stop wasting time on the graphics, fonts, fly-ins, fades and frippery.**

I know you're a bit bored and tired, the movie has finished and there's still a way to go but it's unproductive to muck around with the graphics. Choose a template, sans serif font (easier on the eye), Blue –ish background and something like 24 point minimum. That took 3 minutes. Search your hard drive for suitable images and you're done. Remember 10% of your audience is colour blind and 30-40% have some sort of vision problem requiring contact lenses or glasses, so make it really easy to see. If you see a slide that requires an intro like 'This is a bit hard to read so I'll take you through it….hit 'delete slide'.

3. **Deliver it out loud**

You may baulk at this for fear of social embarrassment but let's look at the options and why it's important. Often the first time the words come out of your mouth is when you're live in front of an audience. Links and key points of your presentation are fluffed because you didn't rehearse.

If you're in Business Class you should be able to stand freely, find a spare metre, plug in your headphones and deliver your presentation out loud. The person in 2B will look at you for a second and then go back to their music or 525 page book on Leadership. Get over it. If you can rehearse your presentation out loud, knowing where the pauses, highlights and key stories are, you will be streets ahead in confidence by the time you get there.

If you're travelling with a colleague, ask them to listen to the presentation. Don't discuss it, defend it or justify why you've put the numbers in first...just deliver it. Get feedback. Review.

4.   Watch it back from the audience's perspective

Consider all members of the audience – key players, influencers, sceptics, hangers-on.

Now, take your presenter hat off and watch the presentation back from each audience member's perspective. Is there something compelling in your 'movie' for each of them? If not, weight the presentation differently so that everyone is included and engaged.

5.   Your physical preparation

If you are literally about to disembark and present, you need to warm up, just like you would for sport. You may not have spoken much on the plane (see: hygiene-challenged seat buddy) or dozed off. Warm up your voice by humming (again, stick the headphones on if you're still worried about the shmuck next to you). Don't drink chilled water or fizzy drinks because it constricts vocal chords and causes hiccups. Choose room temperature water, tea, black coffee and give the booze a miss. (sorry)

When you rehearse professionally, the audience will love and respect you for it, you will have used your travel time wisely and you can pay for the therapy to overcome any of that social awkwardness with your commission on the winning deal.

V

INSIDE THE CLIENT'S HEAD

How to open Pandora's Box

25. LOST IN TRANSITION

'Life is a series of natural and spontaneous changes. Don't resist them; that only creates sorrow. Let reality be reality. Let things flow naturally forward in whatever way they like.'

- Lao Tzu

Recently I was hired to consult on three major pitches, all of which required the client to transition from a longstanding incumbent to the shiny, new supplier.

Unfortunately so many deals are still lost after months of blood, sweat and beers because the new supplier just couldn't get them over the hump.

This is based on a true story I've called 'James in Sales' to help ensure you have the best possible chance of having the client say 'Yep, we're throwing the comfy shoes out and putting yours on.'

James walked past the overgrown front lawn and didn't even notice the front door was already open. His 14 year old daughter was on her way out yet again to a friend's house.

Loosening his tie, he whispered to his wife in the kitchen 'Have you paid the school fees yet?'

It was the third time in 2 years he had failed to win the new accounts he had forecasted to his APAC boss. It's not just baseball that has a three strikes policy. He despaired at the thought of yet another bloody round of soul destroying conversations with recruiters.

James opened the fridge, looking for the remnants of the previous night's bottle of wine and found an Asahi instead. As the brew soothed the back of his throat he agonised again as to why he lost yet another deal.

He had 15 years' experience, won awards and even went on Safari as a top achiever just 3 years ago.

He had managed the CRM, followed the sales methodology he'd been taught, discussed the value proposition and politics of the account with his boss. The technical consultants spent weeks proving the solution worked and he was pretty sure the client had the budget. So, what went wrong...again?

He couldn't write this one off as 'you win some, lose some.'

What James didn't know was that the decision maker, Steve, was a CIO who was more out of his depth than he imagined. He hadn't delivered on three previous projects, was over budget and just had two key resources depart on maternity leave. In addition, he had a child at home who needed more time as he was behind at school with a learning difficulty.

James uncovered the business drivers, budgets and buying processes but he hadn't really had the frank discussion about two key things: Transition and Steve's personal situation.

In the end, as much as Steve wanted new systems, he couldn't commit to the time, head space, process change and responsibility of something new.

He stayed with the status quo and allocated all of his remaining budget to the incumbent.

So, what could James have done?

- Asked the hard questions early and often to uncover Steve's predicament, rather than gloss over the apparent niggling lack of assuredness that Steve exhibited.

- Spent less time using the pre-sales resources and more time using his own CFO or CEO to create peer-to-peer relationships and understanding.

- Asked Steve to commit the budget for all the pre-sales consulting work rather than seeing it as 'free to be in the game.'

- Presented transition in a way that Steve would have seen as easier than he thought with the risk transferred to the vendor as opposed to the scary 19 point transition and assumptions check list that was in the proposal.

- Created a video of his company's key transition people explaining how keen, knowledgeable, well resourced and ready they were to work on the project and how easy they were going make it.

- Arranged an existing senior client to meet Steve for a genuine one-on-one without James.

- Arranged a personalised letter from his CEO to Steve with his personal guarantee of resources and the success of the project.

James could have simply seen Steve and his business for what they really were, rather than what he hoped they'd be.

What would you have done if you were James?

26. WHY SHARK TANK DECISIONS ARE FLAKEY

'To sell is human.'

- Dan Pink

I love our Australian Sharks in Network Ten's *Shark Tank,* and you can learn a lot from their decision making.

Andrew Banks's urbane style appears a second away from saying 'Come, come, Mr. Bond, you get as much pleasure out of making a killing as I do.'

Queensland's Steve Baxter's warmth belies that he looks like the kindly, younger brother of Wolf Creek's Mick Taylor.

Janine Allis's smiling pitch assassinations are masterful and John McGrath quashes the idea that real estate people don't have a heart.

Naomi Simson is the ruby red, crimson, scarlet voice of Aussie common sense

However, these seasoned, successful, single wardrobe wearing multi-millionaires would have you believe that their decisions come down to getting a serious return on their investment based a lot on numbers together with the perceived passion of the business owner.

Perhaps not.

Here's why and the significance for you in your pitches.

Numbers aren't the magic solution.

Putting aside the funsters who couldn't count to 21 unless they were naked, there have been plenty of pitches for reasonable businesses where the requested investment wasn't too high, the presentation was professional and the valuation modest enough to comfort the most anxiety ridden bean counter.

Yet they didn't get a single Shark's money.

Why?

The Sharks couldn't be stuffed working with something not sexy enough. Most people (except for Naomi) thought a business selling Pegs with a hook was about as exciting as visiting your ex-partner's Nanna.

The Sharks have limited time and the cost of mentoring was greater than the raw numbers in the business. Let's face it: Some people could suck the energy out of a room as soon as they walk in.

There have been nine times already when a Shark has said something like 'It would help if you listened.'

(Do your clients think you are coachable or a pain and difficult to deal with?)

The Sharks liked the presenter, but didn't 'loooove them.'

Not fickle; practical, given the amount of time they'll spend together.

So it isn't just about the numbers.

It is or isn't 'Them.'

Janine is drawn to food and beverage businesses like a half price Jimmy Choo sale.

Apart from a weird bottle top thingy, Andrew seems more interested in eating the food than investing in it.

Everyone blinked at a baby showering chair except John McGrath, the Real Estate guy who knows what really happens in rental and new properties.

Even the emotionally charged Disabilities Based Child Care Centre only received two offers out of five because certain Sharks felt they weren't best fit.

If it's not 'them' they won't do it, no matter what the spreadsheet looks like.

So, what does all this mean for your pitches?

Your pitches can learn more from *Shark Tank* than passionate presentation skills and getting the numbers right.

Your clients are like Sharks.

Base camp is getting the numbers of the deal right, the ROI, the cost/benefit story.

Presenting persuasively and engagingly is important but only the next rung up.

The really great pitches tap deep into the history, patterns, egos, personalities and emotional peccadillos of their clients.

Great pitches are steeped in emotionally connected strategies for individuals, not business to business strategy.

Great strategists know that if the client has never bought high end consulting services before, they need to come up with a tonne of proof and comfort to assuage 'we don't normally do this.'

Great pitch leaders have learned how to sell transition from their experience watching deals sour despite making 'business sense' because the client couldn't be stuffed transitioning from one supplier to the other.

Next time you watch *Shark Tank*, note what you think really drove one person's decision over another. Then look at your own upcoming deals and ask yourself about your strategies.

After all, you don't want your new, high potential client saying 'I'm Out.'

27. WHAT'S CHANGED IN SELLING TO PROCUREMENT

'New Procurement is like a squad of Liam Neesons. They have a very special set of skills. They will hunt you down, they will find you and they will kill you.'

– Elliot Epstein

One wag suggested Procurement is the art of pretending not to be the slightest bit interested in buying anything on offer whilst simultaneously being desperate to supply products and services urgently to their own company.

I think it was me.

But Procurement has changed, or at least is well on the way to changing and you should be prepared for it.

Here are a few insights into the new world of selling to procurement.

Harry Halitosis is Dying Out

Harry grew up in purchasing and gravitated to procurement in a fluke restructure where he learned to grow his own dandruff and bark rudely at suppliers who didn't give him what he wanted.

Harry has no vision and his company wouldn't dare give him visibility on their real needs, so he can't make any decisions of note. Handling Harry is simple – go around him and stop being such a Sooki La La about probity and the document that says you can't.

Harry won't buy from you anyway unless you're cheaper than a Cambodian call centre worker.

However, you won't need to stock up on breath mints for Harry for much longer.

He is being replaced by a new breed of Procurement professionals, increasingly female, well-educated and with a broader view of value.

She is also very well educated in the art of negotiation, so you'd better be too.

New Procurement Now Has Real Power

Newer procurement professionals often come with strong lines of business background including Operations, Finance, HR, IT and, would you believe, Sales.

They not only know their supply chain and how it works, but they are also well networked in their industry and can Google faster than your 12 year old when a new app comes out.

To top it off they are given real authority by their senior stakeholders.

If you sell products and services that are classified as Indirect Spend (not material to their core function) like IT, Print, Travel, Labour Hire, Equipment, Professional Services, etc., chances are they have the imprimatur to guide and drive a lot of decisions.

I know of at least two clients that have the Chief Procurement Officer reporting directly to the CEO and are afforded the autonomy accordingly.

Sales 101 cheese, crappy rapport building and talking brochure sales behaviour will fail miserably.

The way you craft your offer and negotiate from there will be critical.

Real case studies as opposed to the new testimonials you have in Alabama or Kazakhstan will be vital.

These procurement people are like a squad of Liam Neesons.

They have a very special set of skills, they will hunt you down, they will find you and they will kill you. You will be 'Taken' in the negotiation if you're not careful, and that means serious margin is at stake, not to mention onerous deliverables.

You Are Always Negotiating

When we run negotiation skills training for sales people it's typically a couple days a year.

(*http://www.salientcommunication.com.au/how-you-can-win-new-business/negotiation-skills-training/*)

Your new procurement friends will spend up to 8 days a year in formal and informal training and certifications.

By the time you've picked up your first double strength ristretto/skinny latte/macchiato, Procurement will have negotiated their first 100k in savings for the day.

You should always have multiple options, tender compliant or outside the scope of the tender – good procurement people will look at it, even if only to pick your brains and leverage the incumbent, if it's not you.

You should implicitly know where you can move and where you can't, and you need a shield as big as the ozone layer to handle all myriad of tactics.

It's a new world. Britain is leaving the EU, rap is still considered music and Procurement is armed, educated and licensed to buy.

This message will self-destruct in 5 seconds.

Together with Paul Rogers, an acclaimed international procurement guru, we have written a book for sellers and buyers, 'Sales Vs Procurement – the Secrets Unveiled at the Negotiation Table' available through Amazon and www.salientcommunication.com.au .

28. WHAT YOUR C-LEVEL CLIENTS REALLY THINK

'All truths are easy to understand once they are discovered; the point is to discover them.'

- Galileo

Have you ever walked out of a meeting with a CEO, CFO or CIO, hit the button on the elevator and thought 'I heard what s/he said but I still don't quite know what makes this person tick'?

Imagine if you could hypnotise them or put truth serum in their short macchiato to learn what they really think.

Well, after years of research and real world examples, I'm going to tell you. It may not be what you think and you need to know to win serious business.

'I'm not an entrepreneur, I'm a corporate executive.'

Most C Suite execs are not Richard Branson.

I have chosen a life of power, status, politics and constant career advancement.

Think Jack Nicholson's Colonel Nathan R Jessep from 'A Few Good Men' when he says to his direct report 'I've been promoted up through the chain of command with greater speed and success than you have. Now if that's a source of tension or embarrassment for you, well, I don't give a sh*t.'

Decisions are made more readily on how it makes me look than how it directly benefits the company. Obviously I'm very adept at juggling both but if push comes to shove.

'I'm inherently sceptical because I've been seriously burnt before.'

As I've risen through the ranks from Finance, Operations, Engineering, IT or Sales in the past 10 or 20 years I've formed very strong opinions on what methods work and what approaches don't.

Like a jilted lover who never forgets getting dumped by their first love, I remember being let down by suppliers, vendors, engineers and sales people who promised the world and delivered Somalia.

While we're in Africa, I also recall the almost Nigerian-scam-like deals that offered cost savings that never materialised and maintenance contracts I was stuck with for years.

After the smell of my burning flesh dissipated I vowed to never again believe in shiny presentation packs, vague promises or people who wear nice suits regardless of the brand on their business card.

I greatly value proof: empirical, financial, demonstrable, referenceable proof and like Honey & Soy Chicken Chips. I don't want one; I want lots.

'I don't always trust my direct reports.'

I have some in my team whose opinions I trust and equally there are a couple of self-serving weasels who just want their favourite suppliers', or worse, my job!

My ego is bigger than theirs and I'm conscious of their agendas when they propose different solutions to our business challenges.

If you are aligned in your bid to the wrong person, you may find yourself in more discomfort than the cast of 'Embarrassing Bodies.'

I value my peer network – other C-level people, fellow professional association members, MBA alumni and people who have delivered for me before.

Get referrals. Don't cold call me with your BS wanting to 'catch up' or share your new widget.

Tell me you've done this in my industry before and I still read letters if they have proof in them. Emails and voicemails are handled by my assistant, DEL.

'I don't like your Sales 101 behaviour.'

I've had people sucking up to me for years, trying to build rapport, asking me leading questions to get me to see their value proposition, crapping on too long about how good their stuff is and inviting me to a lab, site visit, lunch.

I've seen this hundreds of times and have mastered 100 ways to politely dismiss you, or at best shunt you down the food chain.

Talk to me like an equal, not like you just came out of a Sales Academy for Sheep Dipping Sales People.

It's a conversation, not the beginning of your sales cycle. It's not about you, it's about me. Did I mention ego yet?

Share real insights, not product pitches. Don't spend 10 minutes asking me your canned qualification questions or the nauseating 'What keeps you up at night?'

The answer is Viagra if you must know.

Just spend 50 minutes asking questions in a conversational way with proof points along the way.

'I'm looking for my next role now.'

This place is dysfunctional and I've got a corporate career, two kids in private school, a holiday house and an expensive Harley Davidson collection to support.

In addition, two of my MBA buddies have just got plum jobs and I'm smarter than them.

So, when you talk about long term relationship, I laugh to myself because I know 6-12 months here will see me out.

Give me quick wins, introductions into a new network, immediate cost savings so I can milk my bonus, good publicity or a feather in my cap that I can wave around executive recruiters like a World Cup football fan at a Brazilian after party.

That's what I think most of the time. The rest of the time I think about my kids, my health and enjoying life.

I'm just like you, really.

29. CONTACT ELLIOT

If you would like to publish any of these articles in your newsletter, magazine, newspaper, blog, book or other publications, please contact us via our website or by email info@salientcommunication.com.au.

Salient Communication Programs include:

- **Persuasive Presentation Skills**

- **Executive Level Selling**

- **New Business Development**

- **Senior Executive Coaching/Mentoring**

- **Sales/Sales Management Coaching**

- **CEO Level Presentations**

- **Deal/Pitch Consulting**

- **Leadership Coaching**

- **Major Bid/Tender Consulting**

- **Negotiation Skills**

- **Online Video Coaching**

- **Keynote Speeches**

- **Selling to Procurement**

**FOR MORE INFORMATION, VIDEOS, PODCASTS AND
ARTICLES ON SALES AND NEGOTIATION VISIT
WWW.SALIENTCOMMUNICATION.COM.AU**

Also available 'Sales Vs Procurement – The Secrets Unveiled at the Negotiation Table', on Amazon or email info@salientcommunication.com.au for a copy.

CONNECT WITH ELLIOT ON

Email   elliote@salientcommunication.com.au

Twitter   https://twitter.com/Elliot_Salient

LinkedIn https://au.linkedin.com/in/elliotepstein

YouTube http://www.youtube.com/user/ElliotEpstein1

SUBSCRIBE AT

http://WWW.SALIENTCOMMUNICATION.COM.AU

**SO THAT WE CAN LET YOU KNOW OF BOOK
UPDATES.**

www.ingramcontent.com/pod-product-compliance
Lightning Source LLC
Chambersburg PA
CBHW071444180526
45170CB00001B/449